The Forward book of poetry

2012

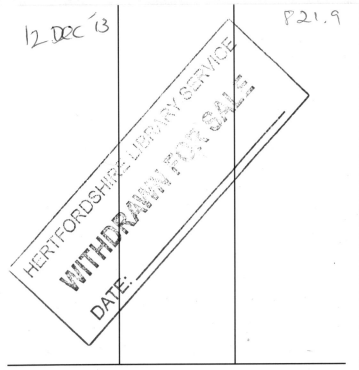

12 DEC '13

P21.9

HERTFORDSHIRE LIBRARY SERVICE

WITHDRAWN FOR SALE

DATE: _____

Please renew/return items by last date shown. Please call the number below:

Renewals and enquiries: 0300 123 4049

Textphone for hearing or
speech impaired users: 0300 123 4041

The Forward Poetry Prizes operate from Forward, one of the UK's leading content agencies. Forward creates beautifully crafted, highly targeted customer communications for clients such as Patek Philippe, Ford, Tesco, Standard Life, Transport for London, Porto Montenegro, Regus and Barclays. Forward's bespoke magazines, websites, ezines and emails are produced in 38 languages and reach customers in 172 countries. For more information, please visit www.theforwardgroup.com

The Forward book of poetry
2012

LONDON

First published in Great Britain by
Forward Ltd · 84–86 Regent Street · London W1B 5RR
in association with
Faber and Faber · Bloomsbury House · 74–77 Great Russell Street ·
London WC1B 3DA

ISBN 978 0 571 27772 8 (paperback)

Compilation copyright © Forward Ltd 2011
Foreword copyright © Andrew Motion

Printed and bound by CPI Group (UK) Ltd, Croydon, CRO 4YY

A CIP catalogue reference for this book
is available at the British Library.

To Jenny Dyson

Contents

Highly Commended Poems 2011

Preface

OVER THE YEARS I'VE OFTEN BEEN ASKED how contemporary poetry
can be made more accessible, and I've usually pointed to initiatives
like National Poetry Day and, of course, the Forward Prizes themselves,
which help bring all kinds of poetry to the widest possible audience.
And who would not want poetry to be open to all? But reading this year's
collection I'm reminded that, on occasions, the very inaccessibility of a
particular poem – its inherent difficulty – forms an integral part of its
power and its allure.

Of course, poetry doesn't have to be difficult, and there's no merit
in difficulty for its own sake. Some of my favourite poems are gloriously
simple, and they're as enjoyable to me now as they were when I was
ten years old. But there's also a great deal of pleasure to be had in
engaging with poems that, at least on first acquaintance, seem remote,
challenging and, yes, apparently inaccessible.

Difficult poems challenge us to engage with them, to think a bit
harder than we're accustomed to. They can be puzzling, obscure,
mysterious. This is exactly what some people dislike about poetry,
what they're objecting to when they ask, 'But what does it *mean*?'
It's a perfectly reasonable question, but then life itself can be baffling
and mysterious, and I admire poets' attempts to capture its sometimes
maddening elusiveness. Puzzles, blurred impressions, faint traces –
they're all to be found among this year's collection, and it's all the
better for that.

Choosing which poems to include is always a challenging task in
itself, so my sincere thanks go to this year's judges, Antonia Fraser,
Sameer Rahim, Leonie Rushforth and Fiona Sampson, stylishly chaired
by Andrew Motion. Supporting them, as always, have been our generous
sponsors: Felix Dennis; Nick McDowell and Arts Council England;
Faber and Faber; the Colman Getty team, including Dotti Irving,
Liz Sich, Kate Wright-Morris, Sarah Watson and Truda Spruyt; and
all at Forward. I hope you enjoy the results.

William Sieghart

Foreword

Since their foundation twenty years ago, the Forward Prizes have become an important and admired part of the literary landscape. Poets care about them because they want to win them; readers care about them because they appreciate their unique interest in giving the sense of a whole year's poetry publishing, rather than simply prizing the achievement of a few individuals. This anthology is a crucial part of the process. As well as containing two poems by every shortlisted author in the Best Collection and Best First Collection categories, and the shortlisted poems in the Best Single Poem section, it also includes work by other poets that impressed the judges (those being Lady Antonia Fraser, Sameer Rahim, Leonie Rushforth, Fiona Sampson and myself).

Inevitably, selection for the anthology is driven partly by the desire to show variety as well as quality: contemporary British poetry is as diverse as contemporary British society, and it's a pleasure to reflect that. At the same time, though, the judges have wanted to show the dominant themes that emerged in the course of our reading. The precarious state of the natural world; the fascinations (and the burdens) of history; the tensions between an individual's need for stability and their fear of (and, sometimes, subversive appetite for) danger: perhaps these are sufficiently large subjects to appear in any annual poetic round-up, but they seemed to loom especially large in this year's offerings.

Our other guiding principles have been more general. The collections we have chosen to shortlist for the prizes, and the additional poems we have chosen for this anthology, caught our eye because they have the capacity to surprise and entertain, while at the same time showing a completely serious engagement with the contemporary world. Saying so appears to imply they are predominantly occupied with the here and now. But that's not what I mean. Continuing British wars, the financial crisis and life under the coalition government were in fact conspicuous by their absence from the submissions. Does this mean their authors have, for one reason or another, deliberately avoided these subjects? Or have they found oblique ways to include them, and made them a part of the other dominant themes on display here?

Readers of the anthology will make their own decisions, and measure the pressure of history in their own ways. But as they do so, I hope they will feel that while the reference points of several poems might seem unspecific, they are not imprecise, and never unfeeling. The longer our deliberations continued, the more apparent it became that the books and individual poems we wanted to honour were those that most tellingly combined their clear-looking and wise-thinking with strong emotion.

Speaking for myself, this made the judging process a long and fascinating reminder that although we might aspire to saying clever things about poems, and might enjoy reading poems that are themselves clever (there are good examples of such things in the pages following), we do poetry a disservice, and deny something vital in its nature, if we forget that it is, in all sorts of important respects, a primitive thing. It appeals at the most fundamental level (as well as the most exalted) to the human animal's appetite for music in words, for rhythmical elaboration and confirmation, and for the point at which sense arrives by a means that has to do with more than merely rational discourse.

The poems in this selection richly illustrate all these qualities – and many more besides. I am very grateful to my fellow judges for sharing them with me – and now with you.

Andrew Motion, *July* 2011

Shortlisted Poems
The Forward Prize for Best Collection

John Burnside

Begin with the fend-for-yourself
of all the loves you learned about
in story books;

fish-scale and fox-print
graven on the hand
forever
          and a tiny hook-and-eye

unfastened in the sweetmeat of a heart
you thought would never grieve
or come undone.

May; and already
it's autumn: broken gold
and crimson in the medieval

beechwoods, where our shadows come and go,
no darker
than the figures in a book

of changes,
till they're hexed
and singled out

for something chill and slender in this world,
more sleight-of-hand
than sorrow or safekeeping.

NATIVITY

I come by chance. A train slows in the fog
and stands a while

and, when it leaves, there's one more soul aboard,
sung from the quiet, passing from car to car,
like the angel of God;

or, north of here, in some old lumber town,
the church clock stops, the wind dies in the trees

and I lie squalling in a slick of blood
and moonlight, seventh son
to some man's seventh son.

No gifts for me, no angel in the rafters
caught like a bird in the updraft from the stove,

only the words of an old curse scratched on the wall,
and the warmth of my mother
fading, as lights go out

in house after house, from here
to the edge of the world,

her slack mouth, then the darkness in her eyes
the first thing I see
when the midwife returns with a candle.

David Harsent

THE LONG WALK TO THE END OF THE GARDEN

The rusty stain on the pillow, the rumble of pain
in your knee, impromptus of a dream in which

you hacked your way out again and again, the dawn
fading up from the green-blue-green of the silver birch,

a flourish on the surface of the pond, a ragged skein
of bindweed on the stone-cold statuette

of that thin-lipped girl from the dream, the odds-on bet
that nothing returns or renews, that the stain

is just what it seems, that the sudden catch
in the throat, the moment of blind regret,

will be all in all, that your way through the garden wet
will take you, for sure, out by the willow-arch

on a morning much like this, and into the lane
beyond which must lie the far field, beyond which

a nameless road, beyond which a landline drawn
in clumsy charcoal below a clumsy sketch

of yourself as pseudocide, a frantic silhouette
soon smudged to shadow by incoming rain.

Rain, midnight rain, nothing but the wild rain
On this bleak hut, and solitude, and me
Edward Thomas, 'Rain'

And here it is, slap on the co-ordinates,
nothing special of course,
a tar-paper roof (is it?) nailed to sloping slats,
a door that's flush to the floor, and grates
when you draw it back. Weather-worn, half-hidden by gorse
in full fire, it being that time of year; the window
thick with cobwebs, clarty candyfloss;
a hint of rot; things spongy underfoot.

Being here alone is easiest.
There are songbirds in the sedge
(I think it is) and a wind to clout the reeds, a test
of the place, as are these clouds: a long dark flow
pulling fast and heavy off the ridge…
Easiest given what we make of quest,
its self-regard, its fearsome lost-and-found, its need to know
the worst and wear its sorrows like a badge.

Do you get what I mean if I speak of light – half-light –
that seems to swarm: a mass
of particles folding and rolling as if you stood too close
to a screen when the image dies? The edge
of night… those forms that catch and hold
just at the brink where it's nearly but not quite.

I see, now, by that light. Rain finally coming in, the day
falling short, adrift in shades of grey,
and nowhere to get to from here, or so I guess,

with distances fading fast,
with the road I travelled by a thinning smudge,
with all that lay between us bagged and sold,
with voices in under the door that are nothing more nor less
than voices of those I loved, or said I did,
with nothing at all to mark
fear or fault, nothing to govern loss,
and limitless memory starting up in the dark.

Geoffrey Hill

13

Don't accost me here on anomalies –
Will Lawes auditioning for Ronnie Scott,
        Alto sax, lute –
        So he survives
        Demi-famous
        The rakish hat
     Musicianship that moves
        Oddly in state.
Why do you so plug *wit and drollery*?
Clop-clip-clop, ups with his troop to Chester
        Unmerrily
        To register,
        To be felled, *slain*,
        Etcetera;
    In what corpse-rift unknown;
      Riffraffed the day.
Lawes makes his way in grinding the textures
Of harmony; so I think, here's a mind
        Would have vexed yours
With late unharpied bounty wrought to find.

        *

What else here fit but mimicked *consort setts*
   Patterns that crown elaborate
    True deliberation
     Fantasies come
      At cost:
      At best
     In crossing rhyme
    Shake a crosspatched nation.
   Small chance factoring at such rate
Wrote finish to, not stasis of, regrets.

There is a noise in my head: the breaking
Of sequence. Have worked to repletion
   Not yet disgust.
   As ever cost-
   Estimates fall
   Short of cost. Still,
  Before sleep, on waking,
   Know the eyes bleed.
Undertaken for honouring the dead
From our nation. Fulfilled in a thrusting
   Forward of rhyme
   Upon a theme
   Long protesting
   Some lame notion
  I had and have: barely
   But entirely
Devoted to those I disregarded,
Who looked to me, then; and no more retain
   The common pain.
From gapped inscripts let them gape recorded.

     *

Trespass and consequence; misrequital;
 Lightly hidden lies equity.
  I shall not reveal how
   Much warmth was spent
   In ice
   Device.
  Is it slight cant
  Wishing to end well? Now
 Good occasion not to pity
Those so barely moved by such recital.

Michael Longley

THE WREN

I am writing too much about Carrigskeewaun,
I think, until you two come along, my grandsons,
And we generalise at once about cows and sheep.
A day here represents a life-time, bird's-foot trefoil
Among wild thyme, dawn and dusk muddled on the ground,
The crescent moon fading above Mweelrea's shoulder
As hares sip brackish water at the stepping stones
And the innovative raven flips upside down
As though for you.
                        I burble under your siesta
Like a contrapuntal runnel, and the heather
Stand that shelters the lesser twayblade shelters you.
We sleepwalk around a townland whooper swans
From the tundra remember, and the Saharan
Wheatear. I want you both to remember me
And what the wind-tousled wren has been saying
All day long from fence posts and the fuchsia depths,
A brain-rattling bramble-song inside a knothole.

CLOUDBERRIES

You give me cloudberry jam from Lapland,
Bog amber, snow-line titbits, scrumptious
Cloudberries sweetened slowly by the cold,
And costly enough for cloudberry wars
(Diplomatic wars, my dear).
                                        Imagine us
Among the harvesters, keeping our distance
In sphagnum fields on the longest day
When dawn and dusk like frustrated lovers
Can kiss, legend has it, once a year. Ah,
Kisses at our age, cloudberry kisses.

D Nurkse

A crèche has been set up
at the crossroads, and above the infant,
right in the manger, the craftsman has placed
the figure of Jesus crucified, as if
night and day exist side by side
like two trees in the dim white forest:
but since noon I've been hearing drumming
and it's a soldier's drum: he might be practicing
or he might be transmitting orders, watching his own hands
become enchanted, become natural. I've smelled smoke
but it might be a charcoal burner in need
of Christmas money: all the same I wish
the drifting snow would hurry and blot out
the Star, the Kings, and the dying man.

My grandmother's flesh has grown luminous,
cloudy behind her nylon housecoat.
Since her treatments, she can keep down
only jello, sherry, and whipped cream.
She stays up all night watching old movies:
sometimes she loses her temper, turns off the sound,
and hexes the characters in a language
no one in this city has heard of: by day
she stares at the Hudson framed in her window.
She can no longer identify the flags of freighters
and asks me to, but strain as I may
my vision blurs, and she insists, so I wind up
inventing nations: Liguria, Phoenicia,
Babylonia… and she nods. On her wall
Kennedy faces Truman but there's no picture
of the child dead of consumption
or the child dead of hunger
or the child who was my father
who succeeded, whose heart failed:
all there is from that world is a locket
showing the infant Mozart playing silence
on a tiny clavichord, behind cracked glass.

Sean O'Brien

Josie

I remember the girl leaning down from the sunlight
To greet me. I could have been anyone. She could not:
She was Josie, remember, and smiling – she knew me already –
Auburn gate-girl to the garden-world,
To the lilacs and pears, the first summer
Seen perfectly once, then never again. And she left.
The garden – the garden, of course, has gone under the stone
And I cannot complain, a half-century gone
Like the cherry tree weeping its resin,
The dry grass, the slab of white marble
The butcher propped up in the back yard to sit on –
Things of the world that the world has no need of,
No more than of Josie or me or that morning.
Still a child as I see now, she leaned down
To smile as she reached out her brown hands to greet me
As though this were how these matters must be
And would be forever amen. She was saying goodbye.
And I cannot complain. What is under the stone
Must belong there, and no voice returns,
Not mine and not hers, though I'm speaking her name.

LEAVETAKING

In memory of Peter Porter

In a draughty terrace bar
Beside the *cave* at Château Ventenac,
And lapped by the green Midi canal,
I take my leave, old friend,
By raising *une pression* and not
The Minervois that you would recommend.
Bad news prefers its poison cold and long.
The news has not improved so far –
So, keep the decent bottle in the rack
For later, for the 'decent interval'
That death like a bureaucracy requires.

Or maybe neck it in the midnight heat
Up at the house when everyone's in bed,
At one end of the huge white tablecloth,
At which a Nazi colonel also sat
To sample the warm south
While waiting for the war to end –
The kind of fact you would absorb
For later, but there is no later now.
Flute-playing psychopaths all must
Like cats and poets come to dust,
But I will not be reconciled.

The evening boats slide in,
Last autumn's leaves still piled
Along their guttering and in the seats
Of plastic chairs left out on deck
In token of a former merriment
In which I am required to believe
When the patron, a rugby star
From some time back, limps past
To put another freezing glass beside the last,

Then fire the oven up with grubbed-up vines
And stand admiring its crimson speech
As though like alcohol it were
A kind of poetry. My friend,
Is there sufficient detail for you yet?
You'd know much faster than I ever could
The point at which the orchestration starts
And evening is converted into art.

La patronne with her brutal crop
And wide-girl suit comes out
To criticize the styling of the blaze.
The grinning barman comes by bicycle
And finds their bickering, the bar,
The voices from the dim canal, the flicker
Of the bunting's spectral tricolores
A stage to serve his wordless drollery:
These are perhaps our characters, but where's
The crowd to fill the choruses
Of black-edged pastoral?

The world, you'd say, exists
Not to be understood
But to demand conviction. I assent,
As if it matters, and the dancers have arrived,
Cool, pink-pastelled blondes who
In another life have raised
A *parapluie* at Cherbourg, squired
By lupine George Chakirises in black.

This is the world, or part of it.
They do not think themselves Shakespearean,
Although you might, were we to sit
Beside the water here, me with *une pression*
And you among the quiet notes you will transform
Into a poem in the high nine hundreds.
I have not learned your lesson yet.

Work is good, like love and company,
But these so-courteous deaths, who sweep
Their maidens up and down the shore
In perfect silence on their light fantastic feet
(When did the music stop?) insist
That they are quite another thing,
Sent from a place less beautiful than this
But just as carefully designed,
The shade beyond the trees and the canal,
Where evening ends, and songs likewise,
And there is no one left to sing.

Shortlisted Poems
The Felix Dennis Prize for Best First Collection

Rachael Boast

FIRE SHOWER

Lying down on a bench by the bridge,
a moon in late Gemini hidden from view,
I think of you who I loved a moment ago
as handfuls of light thrown up in the sky
find the brief flower of their suspension.

They fall so much shorter
than those on-lookers of the upper air;
our old loves, our oarsmen, radiant
in their silence, too steady to take an insult,
too self-possessed to need us.

Lights from regal crescents. Brunel's
ingenious shortcut to the woods
and rockets fired from the observatory roof
leave me cold – my eye's on Jupiter, just visible
through the cloud: *first you see me, now you don't.*

The Hum

*There is not yet a single word, but the poem
can already be heard…*
                                    – Osip Mandelstam

It takes all night to turn the page –
no offence to the poem – its image
sets up so bright a mirror
the room moves towards it, vaster

for all the darkness I'm left sitting in.
By mid-morning you were fathoming
how to decant me from one vessel to another,
his to yours, replace the stopper

and drink. But what you drank was laced
with a distance, like moonlight traced
back to the moon at her most explicit,
so much so you have to listen for it

close to my mouth. Then, in that way you have
when you persist, like a siderostat,
in fixing me in your view,
what I've kept hidden becomes visible to you.

Judy Brown

THE SOUVENIRS

I didn't suss for years. A decade's passed
since I unpacked and put the Chinese lions
on the fireplace, stony-faced and facing me.

At first I couldn't tell the female from the male.
I'm told the lump beneath her paw's her whelp.
In both their mouths are balls you roll; a finger

fits (and not pleasantly) between their teeth.
They often seemed more dragon-like to me
than leonine – huge plated eyes and cursive

avian claws – more so when the red wine reached
the halfway-mark. Today I moved them to the hall.
Their pit-bull snarl, now trained on the front door

breaks over visitors. Repelling things
is what such beasts are for. It all adds up.
Ten years' bad luck. That daily dose of friendly fire.

Two Virgins

The decommissioning ceremony for the former British Royal Naval flagship HMS Invincible has taken place in Portsmouth, Hampshire today... Last month, Invincible undertook a UK tour to celebrate the ship's silver jubilee... It is unlikely that the ship will ever be recommissioned into the Royal Navy. (Wikinews, Wednesday 3 August 2005)

The ship had been in the Falklands when we got down
to the last condom and I was still virgo intacta.
Here comes HMS Invincible, you'd said, in a sort of despair.

I never thought I'd see her – here, as it turned out,
on our Sunday walk down the Thames Path.
Unexpected ex-servicemen waited with borrowed bikes

in air so hot it twitched against the pale horizon.
The flat water simmered like the tropics
and cormorants shrugged out their metal wings.

She'd been moored-up, blotting out Greenwich.
We didn't notice her moving until she was on us,
her smoke dirtying the air, two tugs urging her on.

She sliced the day in half, like a berg calving.
The banks of the Thames sheared back from her hull
as she chugged her way in, splitting our shiny world.

Thirty years too late, she told me what I knew.
Here comes HMS Invincible, you said. It wasn't funny then.
But it is now. I could see how dangerous she was.

The binoculars pulled me swooping like a sea bird
under the vertigo flare of her bow. Then she was gone.
We were old, nursing our brown hands and feet.

Nancy Gaffield

27 KAKEGAWA

High-flying kite breaks
through the edge,
lift greater than weight,
silk and bamboo held
by an invisible hand
and pushed upward

Women stoop in a row of nnnnns,
the mud sucks them down,
they plunge on,
insert the shoots one by one
before blue water hems them in

A child stands with wind
at his back,
unreels string
oops! another kite
escapes the frame,
wind takes it over Mt Akiba,
tengu smiles

Five figures on the bridge
hold onto their hats,
lean into it

A day so beautiful
feels like an absence

That's May for you
everything still
within reach

Yakushi Buddha
holds his right hand in mudra,
sun and moon, his caretakers.

In the canopy crickets sing
a lament of summer's passing.
Sun going down backlights mountain,
birds ribbon lapis-lazuli sky.

Garbed in grey I anchor
on the bank of a shallow river,
an egret settles next to me.
We both stare ahead,
always travellers
in a foreign place.

Those we've left never change.

We talk until the belling
of a temple returns through trees.
When it comes to leaving
you birds are the experts.
Egrets scatter like leaves.

At Ishiyakushi, Buddha of Healing
tells you not to fear.

Moon sweeps the path clean.

Ahren Warner

JARDIN DU LUXEMBOURG

Here, all parks are masculine, grammatically so
I mean: *le jardin, le parc*, never a *la*.
Planes defined by avenues, circulars,
lines on the maps labelled with saints, saintly
politicos: Saint Michel, Kennedy, Jacques.

Even the flowers, here, are masculine;
reminding us of the season, a year or so back,
Gucci, or some such, had men preening
in powder-pink shirts, strutting their cocks
down the Strand, Bishopsgate, Bank.

Here, there are no pink shirts, hardly any
shirts at all. Just men, reclining in the bronze
of their *estomacs*; the vague swell of their guts
rising to the heat. There are women too, of course,
mostly with tops, but tops rolled up,

estomacs bared to the sun. We are reclining too,
squinting at the sky – as electric, if lighter
than Klein's – swallowed up or slipping in
to an igloo of *sérénité*, the gender of which
I've had neither the time, nor desire, to look up.

Though, when it comes to breasts, it's a different story.
Cranach, for example, never seems to have progressed
beyond his pubescent attempts at apprenticeship:

tennis balls sewn to a pillow of hay, fingers coming
to terms with the concept of foreplay. So too
with Titian, whose *Venus* bares handleless plungers

or the fruits of a template mocked up at Bellini's.
For breasts, you want Rochegrosse, his *Chevalier*
surrounded by breasts real enough to have men

gripping their gallery plans discreetly; or Picabia
at his most garish: his naked, peroxidised blonde
stretching to coddle her slavering mutt. Her breasts

impress their tender weight upon us, and though
not as lofty as Pieter would have liked, she too
knows something of our weakness; that we fall

and are floored as much by the salt lure of skin.

John Whale

I will lay to in my most rational method.
At eight and a half I could dissect a dog
and anatomize a pregnant hare.
I did it in the din of my father's shambles,
in the thick stench of his curing yards.
I cherished each dead mare I drained.
I sent hot tallow along the exact course
of all her pink and purple vessels
as if it were the milk of human kindness.
And as she floated from the roof-beam's teagle
I heard her hoof-tips tick the flagged floor.
There was no time to be lost. I undressed
the membranes of her peritoneum and pleura
and relieved her of all her baggy guts and lungs.
I worked in the coldest months with vinegar
and scribbled down notes at every stage.
I have drawn the demon's claws on a filly's back.
I have exposed the human form divine
with that of the tiger and the common fowl.
Now I've removed all trace of boots, bridle
and the pride of the Rockingham Whigs.
At last, I've boiled it down to this:
taut tawny grace on an earthy ground,
pure horse in all its own space.

II

To know the horse I work back to bone.
I will remove the well-groomed mane,
the plaited tail and the ribbon'd fringe.
The velvet flesh of the lower head
sticks tight as any lady's glove.
The skin falls off without demur

this beast so fabulously blue and pink,
its inner coils rippling in the tide,
its lungs like South Sea sponges,
its wasted teeth of revealed coral.
When whalers stand aboard their carcasses
and slice through flesh to fresh baleen
they work their way back down the bone
so that they can distil it all to ambergris:
to light a city's lamps and studios.
And I will assemble the polished bones,
start out now from scratch to find
the invisible genius of the horse.

Lines on the Death of Mary Wollstonecraft

It is twenty minutes before eight.
Downstairs, they lower their voices
and use two hands to open doors.
A plate chinks in the parlour.
A broom is sweeping the yard.
Fires flare silently into life
and the very air is muffled
with a clear understanding.
Objects in the grey room take on
the familiar shape of objects.
Outside, the cabs and carriages
on their way through the dust
rattle the cobbles with a sound
which is neither midsummer
nor the dead of winter.
In the room below, light
breaks like a stick of chalk
on a table set for two.

Room after room, door after door,
I search the house through
and come up with nothing.
Nothing touched it seems by her
as she went reeling through life.
And it took so many days to die.
I take her brave book of letters
which suits this frozen north
that grips the edges of my mind.
Her spirit melts happiness
to nothing less than true content.
Through my gloom of innumerable pines
a waterfall jumps the darkness
and its voice suddenly aches,
aches with a weight of water

flowing under Putney Bridge.
I imagine her ghostly skirt
billowing in the cold Norwegian sea.

But she is striking out for life
alone on the wide ocean.
Before her floats a veil or gauze,
a cold transparent envelope
of water thickened into life
and marked for life with rings
like bloodstains in the snow.
It trails purple ribbons.
As my tears salt the sparkling waves
I begin to see through her bright I
as it meets the cold light of day.
Somewhere in the near distance,
a new-born baby starts to cry.
It is twenty minutes before eight.

Nerys Williams

The Dead Zoo, Dublin

for John Peel

I

In the dead zoo we walk an afternoon
touching the giraffe with a sutured stomach

and the bull seal with a broken ear.
The gazelles too are thinking

about the jungle kings, sun-kissed and light-bleached
making a performance of their anger.

All hips and grimaces the hyenas
pass silent commentary on our clothes.

And I remember finding the bat in daylight
on the schoolyard wall, its cape and hooks

trembling, broken by the colourwash of light,
it hated being stroked.

We had a bat funeral, a ceremony that summer
which followed other rituals:

wreath laying for road kill, bouquets for robins
and elegies for tame jackdaws.

strange to find oneself here with these exhibitionists
teasing us that they are alive still.

2

Music is a skin,
notes at the tips of my fingers
fingertips at the edge of my song.

After the elegies and the websites
after the obituaries and the radio stories
after the musicians and magazines
after the bulletins and the brouhaha
there was nothing left but teenage kicks.

3

So I take you to the dead zoo
your own private Gethsemane
to curate the animals into action.

4

I will use your words against mine with mine and on mine,
I will play all your records at the same time

the unreleased singles and demos
causing cacophony on the dance floors.

Rhythm is a bright confusion
I will say that music is homesickness

And you can give me your *unheimlich*
as an elegy of recognition.

Loie Fuller's Dancing School

I am terpsichorean
a figure in burlesque.

Sometimes Miss Pepper stranded on the prairie
sometimes Buffalo Bill's navvy
sometimes a soubrette.

Imagine my surprise at the spectacular
a bijou opera house.

An alien in melodrama
Aladdin-girl in melos.

In the cave of the fire of life,
I am Ayesha of two thousand years

finding a silhouette
within slimness.

Such methods of the divine
becomes a gal from Chicago.

Shortlisted Poems
The Forward Prize for Best Single Poem

Alan Jenkins

SOUTHERN RAIL (THE FOUR STUDENTS)

That left-over halt… It's where, years ago,
Four of us at the end of our student days
Got out and walked for hours in midsummer heat
Down lanes and bridle paths and unmarked ways
Through waist-high grasses, warmth-holding wheat;

Or let the river lead us, full and slow,
Past stands of willow, clumps of oak and beech
And their reflections that one dazzling swan
Sailed across – above that wide green reach,
Cloudless blue. To think: only one-third gone

Of life! Two boys, two girls, still owed a living each;
Two of us in love, all four the most free
We'd ever be, with nothing more in mind
Than the next pub and no-one more inclined
To ask where we were going than the other three.

Yet it wasn't like the world I knew I'd find,
Cocksure, twenty-one and walking
Towards my smiling future with no fear
Except of what I didn't want, and no idea
I'd talked it to death – while death was stalking

One of us, in fact: though we could not know.
He's gone now. I stood still, while the others
(*Like some I might have…*) went where they had to go,
Went to be wives (and one a widow), mothers…
This time the river's just as sluggish-high,

The fields and farmhouses in their stands of trees
Are as perfect as that day; but now *Too late*,
They say, *for you to taste seclusion, ease,*
The beauty you see here. From the crossing-gate
We have, to one who knows he too will die,

The look of permanence, of hallowed ground
You cherish since you've grasped it will remain
Almost the same when you are not around
To gaze at it. And this new kind of pain
Goes with you as you sit in the London train,

As you walk from your station up the hill
Past playground, car-park, pub... Not many lights
Left on at this hour. Some, sleepless still,
Pace their rooms, their minds full of other nights;
One smokes, arms folded on a windowsill;

One tinkers on the internet; one reads.
In piss-smelling tunnels, wire-fenced alleyways,
On paving stones that sprout stubborn weeds
The streetlamps' slick, repeated orange blaze
Points the way home. I know where it leads.

R F Langley

To a Nightingale

Nothing along the road. But
petals, maybe. Pink behind
and white inside. Nothing but
the coping of a bridge. Mutes
on the bricks, hard as putty,
then, in the sun, as metal.
Burls of *Grimmia*, hairy,
hoary, with their seed-capsules
uncurling. Red mites bowling
about on the baked lichen
and what look like casual
landings, striped flies, *Helina*,
Phaonia, could they be?
This month the lemon, I'll say
primrose-coloured, moths, which flinch
along the hedge then turn in
to hide, are Yellow Shells not
Shaded Broad-bars. Lines waver.
Camptogramma. Heat off the
road and the nick-nack of names.
Scotopteryx. Darkwing. The
flutter. Doubles and blurs the
margin. Fuscous and white. Stop
at nothing. To stop here at
nothing, as a chaffinch sings
interminably, all day.
A chiff-chaff. Purring of two
turtle doves. Voices, and some
vibrate with tenderness. I
say none of this for love. It
is anyone's giff-gaff. It
is anyone's quelque chose.
No business of mine. Mites which

ramble. Caterpillars which
curl up as question marks. Then
one note, five times, louder each
time, followed, after a fraught
pause, by a soft cuckle of
wet pebbles, which I could call
a glottal rattle. I am
empty, stopped at nothing, as
I wait for this song to shoot.
The road is rising as it
passes the apple tree and
makes its approach to the bridge.

Sharon Olds

Song the Breasts Sing to the Late-in-Life Boyfriend

When you touch them, their skin feels like the surface
of a soap bubble, tensile and shimmering,
the oils of many colors moving
in swirls, like the Coriolis winds of the globe.
When you hold them, it feels as if, within each,
there's a solar system, majestic, lawful,
playful. When you hold one in your grip, a moment –
gently, but not sentimentally, and
shake it, there starts to snow a flurry
in my chest and belly, and lower belly,
where the flakes settle and sparkle. And when you
touch their centers, the tips of my ears grow
points, when your fingers nip their centers in the
bud, the blood flowers of engorgement
blossom. I like that you like that one of the
stem-stubs will sometimes draw inside, into
its hill, like an ostrich bloom which blooms,
lover of the dark, down into the ground.
When you hold them I feel like plunder adored
which adores being plundered. The mouths of your hands
honor the food of my flesh in its season,
and if it were reasonable to thank you
for doing what you like, I would thank you within reason,
but as it is not, I thank you beyond reason.

Jo Shapcott

Bees

I Tell the Bees

He left for good in the early hours with just
one book, held tight in his left hand:
The Cyclopedia of Everything Pertaining
to the Care Of the Honey-Bee; Bees, Hives,
Honey, Implements, Honey-Plants, Etc.
And I begrudged him every single et cetera,
every honey-strainer and cucumber blossom,
every bee-wing and flown year and dead eye.
I went outside when the sun rose, whistling
to call out them as I walked towards the hive.
I pressed my cheek against the wood, opened
my synapses to bee hum, I could smell bee hum.
'It's over, honies,' I whispered, 'and now you're mine.'

The Threshold

I waited all day for tears and wanted them, but
there weren't tears. I touched my lashes and
the eyewater was not water but wing and fur
and I was weeping bees. Bees on my face,
in my hair. Bees walking in and out of my
ears. Workers landed on my tongue
and danced their bee dance as their sisters
crowded round for the knowledge. I learned
the language too, those zig-zags, runs and circles,
the whole damned waggle dance catalogue.
So nuanced it is, the geography of nectar,
the astronomy of pollen. Believe me,
through my mouth dusted yellow
with their pollen, I spoke bees, I breathed bees.

The Hive

The colony grew in my body all that summer.
The gaps between my bones filled
with honeycomb and my chest
vibrated and hummed. I knew
the brood was healthy, because
the pheromones sang through the hive
and the queen laid a good
two thousand eggs a day.
I smelled of bee bread and royal jelly,
my nails shone with propolis.
I spent my days freeing bees from my hair,
and planting clover and bee sage and
woundwort and teasel and borage.
I was a queendom unto myself.

Going About With the Bees

I walked to the city carrying the hive inside me.
The bees resonated my ribs: by now
my mouth was wax, my mouth was honey.
Passers-by with briefcases and laptops
stared as bees flew out of my eyes and ears.
As I stepped into the bank the hum
increased in my chest and I could tell the bees
meant business. The workers flew out
into the cool hall, rested on marble counters,
waved their antennae over paper and leather.
'Lord direct us.' I murmured, then felt
the queen turn somewhere near my heart,
and we all watched, two eyes and five eyes,
we all watched the money dissolve like wax.

CCD

My body broke when the bees left,
became a thing of bones
and spaces and stretched skin.
I'd barely noticed
the time of wing twitch
and pheromone mismatch
and brood sealed in with wax.
The honeycomb they
left behind dissolved
into blood and water.
Now I smell of sweat and breath
and I think my body cells
may have turned hexagonal,
though the bees are long gone.

The Sting

When the wild queen leads the swarm
into the room, don't shut the door on them,
don't leave them crawling the walls, furniture
and books, a decor of moving fuzz. Don't go off
to the city, alone, to work, to travel underground.
The sting is no more *apis mellifera*, is a life
without honey bees, without an earful of buzz
an eyeful of yellow. The sting is no twin
waving antennae breaking through
the cap of a hatching bee's cell. The sting
is no more feral hive humming in the stone
wall of the house, no smell of honey
as you brush by. No bees will follow, not one,
and there lies the sting. The sting is no sting.

Highly Commended Poems

2011

Fergus Allen

Cloud

Where yesterday were twites and meadow pipits,
Piping in passing, today in damp silence
Cumulus cloud presses down like a pillow
On the upturned face of the heathery hill.
Sometimes the air is lucid and one sees
The town spread on either side of the river
Like the barbs on the rachis of a feather,
Ripe for preening by some almighty bill.

Its belfries and steeples, tailored to advertise
The presence of a living God, lift up
Their long bony fingers into a void
Abandoned by despairing seraphim.
But now the mist enfolds me like a duvet –
As comforter, incubator of fantasy,
Also protector from the Evil Eye.
My vision's gathered in a veil of scrim.

If this is a preview of the afterlife,
It passes quickly and the spiky city
Reasserts itself; below is the river
Over which herring gulls shamelessly yell
While circling slowly in figures of eight.
Mute swans drift with all the time in the world
And the citizens stare at the hills, crying
Look! look! the cloud has lifted, all will be well.

Eavan Boland

Re-reading Oliver Goldsmith's 'The Deserted Village' in a Changed Ireland

1

Well not for years – at least not then or then.
I never looked at it. Never took it down.
The place was changing. That much was plain:
Land was sold. The little river was paved over with stone.
Lilac ran wild.
Our neighbours opposite put out the *For Sale* sign.

2

All the while, I let Goldsmith's old lament remain
Where it was: high on my shelves, stacked there at the back –
Dust collecting on its out-of-date, other-century, superannuated pain.

3

I come from an old country.
Someone said it was past its best. It had missed its time.
But it was beautiful. Blue suggested it, and green defined it.
Everywhere I looked it provided mirrors, mirror flashes, sounds.
Its name was not Ireland. It was Rhyme.

4

I return there for a moment as the days
Wind back, staying long enough to hear vowels rise
Around the name of a place.
Goldsmith's origin but not his source.
Lissoy. Signal and sibilance of a river-hamlet with trees.

5

And stay another moment to summon his face,
To see his pen work the surface,
To watch lampblack inks laying phrase after phrase
On the island, the village he is taking so much care to erase.

6

And then I leave.

7

Here in our village of Dundrum
The Manor Laundry was once the Corn Mill.
The laundry was shut and became a bowling alley.
The main street held the Petty Sessions and Dispensary.

8

A spring morning.
A first gleam of sunshine in Mulvey's builder's yard.
The husbands and wives in the walled graveyard
Who brought peace to one another's bodies are not separated.
But wait. Mulvey's hardware closed down years ago.
The cemetery can't be seen from the road.

9

Now visitors come from the new Town Centre,
Built on the site of an old mill,
Their arms weighed down with brand names, bags.

10

Hard to know which variant
Of our country this is. Hard to say
Which variant of sound to use at the end of this line.

11

We were strangers here once. Now
Someone else
Is living out their first springtime under these hills,
Someone else
Feels the sudden ease that comes when the wind veers
South and warms rain.
Would any of it come back to us if we gave it another name?
(Sweet Auburn loveliest village of the Plain.)

Alan Brownjohn

His Classic Modesty

This is my bedroom, he says in a casual voice,
And lo, my bed, below my photograph
Of the Acropolis. (*My love-making,* he thinks,
And sometimes even dares to say all this out loud
Is like the Acropolis, an edifice
Wonderful to have experienced even once,
And transformative *to have known for a little longer.*
Sufficient of the Acropolis remains
In its incomparable magnificence
To stir a sensitive girl for years to come.
Those who forego it weep at what they have missed
When their chance has vanished. And then he adds
Intelligent girls adore *the Acropolis.*)

Diane Cockburn

Electric Mermaid in Bell's Fish and Chip Shop

She's glowing puffed up neon in the batter tank,
crackling angry,
frying light bulbs,
fusing fluorescent tubes
and screwing eyes round in sockets,
giving customers electric shocks.

Flicking her tail in and out of batter,
she hot hisses
into the vat of mushy peas,
her hair a scurrying mane
of current blips.
She's flirting with fresh haddock,
experimenting with crispy breadcrumbs.
Regulars settle for chips.

Owner, closing early,
shifts his cod pieces and twitches the rubber apron
to protect his assets.
Down on the docks men snigger,
well shot of her, mending
their scorched nets, nursing
fourth degree burns.

At midnight she breaks free in a shower of sparks.
Electrocutes a *Tesco* trolley and is away down Silver Street.
No one stops her, as she plugs into the River Wear.

Touch me baby. Touch me baby blue eyes shrivelled burnt eyes if you dare!

Turning water into fire,
she will make contact with submarines,
using radar love and no earth.
Her electric tattoos sparkle messages to divers.

Burn,
Burn,
Pretty sailors…

Wendy Cope

> *...places of transit where we are aware*
> *of a particular kind of alienated poetry.*
> – Alain De Botton

In the Wimpy Bar at Stafford services
I ask for ketchup. The girl gives me a sachet.
She seems nice, so I mention the red plastic tomatoes
That used to be on every table in the old days.
She has never heard of them. She thinks
Ketchup on the tables is a good idea.

The red plastic tomatoes, the formica tables
In the Wimpy Bar by Barnehurst bus depot
Where I went, aged thirteen, to smoke,
Drink coffee and feel sophisticated.
It was all so modern, so American, so young,
And a safe haven from parents.

Fifty years on I'm sitting in another one,
Drinking coffee and not smoking.
As the light fades the glass walls turn into mirrors,
Lending the place an air of glamour. I like it here.
I could be in an Edward Hopper painting,
A woman travelling alone on business.

No-one knows anything about me. Perhaps
I'm a high-powered executive with a BMW
Outside in the car park. Or some kind of artist,
A poet, maybe, scribbling in her notebook.
Dreams in a Wimpy. I finish my coffee,
Find my keys, and walk out of the picture.

Ian Duhig

THE ORIGIN OF PESTILENCE
Kalevala VL

Loviatar, worst daughter of Death,
half-blind virgin, darker with pain,
with the mother of all pain: birth:

she curses, cold clawing her bones,
in the road, her first childbed; curses
her womb's ninemoonsworth of strife.

Her tears steam and hiss; teeth crack;
she flies up to a gap between crags
to hang for help from gravity's drag,

back down for hot springs; into snow,
then a cataracts' back-breaking force;
none any help. Sky rings with her din.

At last God orders this grievous girl
to North Farm, its hag to midwife her,
freeing her foetus for mischief abroad.

There, in a hovel encircled by bogs,
to birthing charms droned by a witch
Loviatar opens, drops us her dread load.

Michael Egan

THREE ITALIANS AND A SPANIARD

the night before they left   my keys   dug into a beam
carved out *amato* four times   sat finishing the punch
this vision of christmas in wool   fat santa stretched across
his chest   poked my stomach   said *winnie winnie*
that creased him   cried now *mr university will come find me*
he say luigi   *luigi you buy new beams*   the chair
unsteady   cut my name next to his   earlier the spaniard
had been throwing stones at her window   *lara lara*
he sang her name   me in her bed   her too –
toned legs   ran everyday   could have crushed me
lara lara he went on all night   I remembered his story
on the bank of the seine   a communist thespian   his father
pushed de gaulle or mitterrand   someone   into the river
never allowed into france again   how many
parts did he miss out on for that?   it worked out all right
ended up in an iberian *confessions of a window cleaner*
horny matador   randy conquistador
now   the third italian wore too much make-up
like some roman street whore byron might have knocked
and watching her take that paint off was   to watch
a woman undress   naked she wasn't the same
more like the picture her sister took   in the south
she must have been sixteen   naked   so you saw nothing
she burst in   the spaniard was climbing up   calling calling
had woken her   drunk romeo   juliet's hand on my crotch
bursting in   she was shocked   going after her
santa pulled me into the kitchen   poured me another punch
cried about his sweet shop in the mountains   next morning
the italians left for amsterdam   and I spent two weeks
playing black jack   drinking four euro bordeaux with the spaniard.

Mark Ford

Is the night
Chilly and dark? The night is chilly
But not dark. An all but full
April moon
Slides above barely visible clouds, and is greeted
By a burst of hooting from an urban
Tawny owl. On empty
Brownfield sites they nest, and rear their young, and feed
On vermin. Has
Any
Probing, saucer-eyed astronomer, even a modern
Or French one, ever
Grown genuinely accustomed *'aux profondeurs du grand
Vide céleste'*? Someone halts, and broods
In the deserted doorway of a Chinese
Emporium, someone
Is struggling to rise swiftly
From his chair.

*

A pair of empty
Curly brackets might have been
His colophon, I thought, parting one night
At closing time
On Great Russell Street, outside our last port of call,
    the Museum
Tavern. Between his thick-
Soled hiking boots rested a battered duffel bag with a
    single yellow
Shin pad protruding. A group
Of youthful party-goers sashayed by – one wearing a
    traffic cone

On her head: '*like*
A complete unknooown,' a voice from the pack
Intoned… I was picturing the shiny black
Cab he so imperiously
Hailed whisking him west, revving, cruising, braking, gliding
Across junctions, the driver
At length twisting around, awaiting payment, as I veered
And tacked through the eerily silent
Squares of Bloomsbury, towards Euston.

Annie Freud

LUST

for Brian Maguire

You said you'd never been in love but that lust is wonderful,
and repeated the word several times... *Lust... Lust...*
with your eyes shining. You said it was not about the right
woman but something to do with your personality. You
asked me what being in love means; I said it was feeling
wonderful when the person you're in love with is in the
same room with you, that it has a childish aspect, and that
your heart beats faster when you think about them or say
their name, and that you feel a bit crazy and you want to
have sex all the time and keep changing your clothes and
you can't get on with your life or settle to anything, that
you want them to stop talking to other people and only
talk to you.

Then you looked at the rows of bottles and the bunches
of hops hanging from the ceiling and, spreading your
fingers along the counter, you said that if a gunman came
into the bar right now, you were prepared to lose your life
to save the lives of other people, even if you didn't know
them, or love them, or have the slightest interest in them.
And yesterday when I saw you again, you said that if any
of these other people, whose lives you'd be willing to save
from a killer, tried to kill me, you'd kill them without a
second thought.

Lavinia Greenlaw

The Drip Torch

How I fetched up there we do not say.
A land far west and south of myself
so blatant in its growing and dying
clearance was undertaken by fire.
The night after a prescribed burn
you led us through your woods
to a place, strangely enough, of sleep.
The smoke low and still,
a lull of ash and the air a fleece
into which the last weak flames
knitted themselves then disappeared.
As if some great truth had occurred
and we could rest now. How glad I was
when you handed me the drip torch
and taught me how to tend fire
like a gardener with a swing of the can
over anything left untouched,
each soft splash igniting white
as a conjuror's dove
floating down into the earth
making safe the black path.

Kelly Grovier

The Guest

Think of it this way: every time we leave,
someone enters – silent, invisible –
until the house is filled

with the unseen. 'Ghosts make perfect
house guests,' my shadow mutters,
sweeping the floor. Midnight,

and the beds are crumpled with the loss
of piled coats; bloodshot
the eyes of empty wine glasses. Outside,

a taxi idles in the dark. Its door is open.
Honestly, sometimes I can't tell
if I'm coming or going.

Fawzi Karim

AT THE GARDENIA'S ENTRANCE

In front of the Gardenia's bolted entrance,
A middle-aged man with the look of someone who has retired
    is waiting.
I am also a middle-aged man, just returned from exile.
I squat a few feet from him,
And without wasting much time, I ask:
    'Do you know when it opens?'
'The Gardenia Bar was my hangout before the war.
I used to have my own corner there
    with my friends around me.
After the war, it folded, got forgotten.
But I have been coming here for a long time
    waiting cach day for its door to open.'

He stretched a hand out, holding a rolled cigarette,
And I stretched a hand to take it
And smoke spread, blurring the two men
    waiting at the bolted door
On the sidewalk of Abu Nuwas Street.

August Kleinzahler

I

The Super Chief speeds across the American West.
Herr Doktor Doktor Von Geist pulls the ends of his moustache,
almost like a seabird
manoeuvring his wings in unsettled weather,
while he gazes out at the desolation and tumbleweed –
the *echo-less-ness*, as that bore Krenek likes to put it –
moon drifting in and out of the clouds.
With a formal solemnity, confused, perhaps with dignity,
along with the deliberateness of a surgeon,
he runs his fork through the orange emulsion
covering his salad,

               or what they call here salad.
– *Anything wrong, sir*? asks the black waiter,
who, the Doktor notes,
bears more than a passing resemblance to Louis Jordan;
that would be Louis Jordan of jump band fame,
not the other.

II

Door ajar to the great actress's cabana at Nazimova's Garden of Allah,
she lies back on her chaise longue,
gently running a finger along her glistening auburn lanugo,
while, at the same time, changing stations on the radio
until she arrives at *Amos and Andy*, her favourite:
    – *Holy Mackerel, dere, Andy*!
– *Ha, ha, ha, ummmmm*, die Schwartzen…
Just then, Tadzio walks past,
angelic boy in his sailor suit, right off the page,
the *plage*, still shaking sand off,
and catches a glimpse of Frau Lola,
pleasuring herself in anticipation of a visit from Salkia,

or the English tennis star, or, God forbid, Harpo.
But no, it is Tadzio, lovely Tadzio,
Who neither blushes nor even seems taken aback.
– *Mochtest du Pussy essen?*
she asks in a childish voice
                              – *Smeckt gut…*
But the boy's German is imperfect.
Besides which, he has plans for the afternoon.

III

The second, or is it the third, Mrs H.,
consort of the distinguished foreign character actor,
wrinkles her nose,
as if downwind of a giant log of baking *Leiderkranz.*
From high on a stage of his own imagining,
and looking out upon the *mausoleum of easy going,*
the Revolutionary Playwright
in his tailored denim Worker's costume
loads up and begins cranking away,
                              the Gattling Gun of Wilshire Boulevard:

        Francis Assisi at an aquarium
        Chrysanthemums in a coal mine
        Lenin at the Prater
        Tahiti in Metropolitan Form

– *Are we done yet, darling?*
she asks, slowly removing her husband's hand
from the smoking weapon.

IV

Nietzsche, playing his second shot
on the dogleg par 5 eighth at Bel Air,
shanks it into the creek.
                              – *You are a great man,*
Freddy, my boy, a great, great man,

his celebrated playing partner, the misanthropic jokester, intones.
The philosopher stands there, motionless, stricken,
his mutton chops and jowls sinking into the collar
of his powder blue Dacron golf shirt:
dismay, terror, puzzlement, the call of an unfamiliar bird?
                              – No great tragedy
Herr Schickelgruber, a mere bump in the road, bump in the road,
knocking a bee off his plus fours with an antique mashie.

Gwyneth Lewis

(for A J)

X marks the spot where the body went under
The Channel's quilt, whose mighty tides
Rise twice a day. X marks a fetch

As language keeps coming but not the words
For X who was ours but is forever now
Anonymous, and X is how

The surge is lifted by the nursemaid moon
So earth can turn under it, an invalid rolled
Beneath a coverlet. X for the pain

We never located but would have exchanged
For Stay, Be Patient and We Understand
Though we didn't and, finally, X is the link

Of pressure with weather, a final lack
So utter that the slap and suck
Of water was better. Kiss-kiss, kiss-kiss.

Tim Liardet

'...LAY THEE DOWN'

It came back to me quite suddenly – carrying with it the curl
and doubling-back of undertow, things said
in ignorance and later forgotten –
the day the curtains, brother, closed you away

and we stood chewing grief like rinsed lettuce.
Every night for as long as you and I shared
that back room – I said it to you;
loving the sound of the words which played out

excesses I could never quite put to sleep,
I said it, over and over again:
for the last time now goodnight, Davy;
for the last time now goodnight, Davy.

Peter McCarey

Glyph

Rain on a pond somehow becomes
piano improvisation
a sparrow swoops to the kerb on a cosine
dimpled air and feathered oars
the water has cut a heart shape in the rock
more even than my heart
no formula no cardioid curve
this is where proprioception
touches itself and falters
intention focuses
and burns its object sun on paper
smoke on sunlight written out
in words
in other words
to cross from see to say
is not enough
and incoherence
will catch my heel whenever I lose the way
from me to you.

David Morley

CAMARGUES

I will wake up in a world that hooves have led to
                              – Les Murray

Some horses are caves; you catch
that by the way they flicker and shy
at shadow. You can walk inside horses
and sense their walls trembling around you.
Camargues are air-delvers, the pile-driver
we're gripping on our reins, chiselling
granite miles. We caught their backs like luck
then held on. Camargues are not cave,
but they passed through like wraiths
slamming silently through the walls.

Thug-faced, hog-necked, anvil-hoofed
Camargues – necking the paint's hay
on cave walls of Niaux and Lascaux;
cantering behind the wasted warriors
of Rome, Persia and Greece. We rode
them here – or they rode us, chests thumped
out like wagons heaving our wagons;
warmed to our genius grandfathers
because they whispered to them
in horse and only in horse.

We should as well cremate ourselves
alongside our Camargues, riding them
through heaven's walls, hoofed pyres
to our Saints Mary Jacobe and Mary Salome.
We might have fired our horses
on our deaths as we fired our houses;

burnt ourselves upon the deaths
of our horses since we were their houses.
All horses are spells, but Camargues
are myth. You catch that on horseback.

Les Murray

HIGH-SPEED BIRD

At full tilt, air gleamed –
and a window-struck kingfisher,
snatched up, lay on my palm
still beating faintly.

Slowly, a tincture
of whatever consciousness is
infused its tremor, and
ram beak wide as scissors

all hurt loganberry inside,
it crept over my knuckle
and took my outstretched finger
in its wire foot-rings.

Cobalt wings, shutting on beige
body. Gold under-eye whiskers,
beak closing in recovery
it faced outward from me.

For maybe twenty minutes
we sat together, one on one,
as if staring back or
forward into prehistory.

Daljit Nagra

A Black History of the English-Speaking Peoples

I

A king's invocations at the Globe Theatre
spin me from my stand to a time when boyish
      bravado and cannonade
and plunder were enough to woo the regal seat.

That the stuff of Elizabethan art and a nation
of walled gardens in a local one-up manship
      would tame the four-cornered
world for Empire's dominion seems inconceivable.

Between the birth and the fire and rebirth of the Globe
the visions of Albion led to a Rule Britannia
      of trade-winds-and-Gulf-Stream
all-conquering fleets that aroused theatres

for lectures on Hottentots and craniology,
whilst Eden was paraded in Kew.
      Between *Mayflower* and *Windrush*
(with each *necessary murder*) the celebrated

embeddings of imperial gusto where jungles
were surmounted so the light of learning be spread
      to help sobbing suttees
give up the ghost of a husband's flaming pyre.

II

So much for yesterday, but today's time-honoured
televised clashes repeat the flag of a book burning
      and May Day's Mohican
Churchill and all that shock and awe

that brings me back to Mr Wanamaker's Globe.
An American's thatched throwback to the king
          of the canon! I watch the actor
as king, from the cast of masterful Robeson.

The crowd, too, seem a hotchpotch from the pacts
and sects of our ebb and flow. My forbears played
          their part for the Empire's quid
pro quo by assisting the rule and divide of their ilk.

Did such relations bear me to this stage?
Especially with Macaulay in mind, who claimed the passing
          of the imperial sceptre would highlight
the imperishable empire of our arts…

So does the red of Macaulay's map run through
my blood? Am I a noble scruff who hopes a proud
          academy might canonise
his poems for their faith in canonical allusions?

Is my voice phoney over these oft-heard beats?
Well if my voice feels vexatious, what can I but pray
          that it reign Bolshie
through puppetry and hypocrisy full of gung-ho fury!

III

The heyday Globe incited brave new verse
modelled on the past, where time's frictions
          courted Shakespeare's corruptions
for tongue's mastery of the pageant subject. Perhaps

the Globe should be my muse! I'm happy digging
for my England's good garden to bear again.
          My garden's only a state
of mind, where it's easy aligning myself with a 'turncoat'

T. E. Lawrence and a *half-naked fakir* and always
the groundling. Perhaps to aid the succession
             of this language of the world,
for the poet weeding the roots, for the debate

in ourselves, now we're bound to the wheels
of global power, we should tend the manorial
             slime – that legacy
offending the outcasts who fringe our circles.

        IV

Who believes a bleached yarn? Would we openly
admit the Livingstone spirit turned Kurtz, our flag
             is a union of black and blue
flapping in the anthems of haunted rain…?

Coming clean would surely give us greater distance
than this king at the Globe, whose head seems cluttered
             with golden-age bumph,
whose suffering ends him agog at the stars.

        V

I applaud and stroll toward Westminster,
yet softly tonight the waters of Britannia bobble
             with flotillas of tea and white gold
cotton and sugar and the sweetness-and-light

blood lettings and ultimately red-faced Suez.
And how swiftly the tide removes from the scene
             the bagpipe clamouring
garrisons with the field-wide scarlet soldiery

and the martyr's cry: *Every man die at his post!*
Till what's ahead are the upbeat lovers who gaze
             from the London Eye
at multinationals lying along the sanitised Thames.

Bernard O'Donoghue

Each cold October morning he went out
into the Gate Field and walked up and down,
like the horse-drawn seed-drill quartering every inch
to make sure the harvest was kept constant,
reading his Office, every Latin sentence
of the forty pages for the day. In the evening,
as the colder darkness fell with the crows'
harsh calling, he sat alone in the back
benches of the unheated chapel, hour
after hour, staring for inspiration
at the golden, unresponsive tabernacle.

Ian Pindar

WHAT IS THE MATTER?

What is the
matter?

To speak of
matter

To speak in
matter

matter-word
word-matter

in matter
matter speaks
the Word

Clare Pollard

THE CARAVAN

We were alive that evening, on the north Yorkshire moors,
in a valley of scuffed hills and smouldering gorse.
Pheasants strutted, their feathers as richly patterned
as Moroccan rugs, past the old Roma caravan –
candles, a rose-cushioned bed, etched glass –
that I'd hired to imagine us gipsies
as our bacon and bean stew bubbled,
as you built a fire, moustached, shirt-sleeves rolled.
It kindled and started to lick, and you laughed
in your muddy boots, there in the wild –
or as close as we can now get to the wild –
skinning up a joint with dirty hands, sloshing wine
into beakers, the sky turning heather with night,
the moon a huge cauldron of light,
the chill wind blasting away our mortgage,
emails, bills, TV, our broken washing machine.
Smoke and stars meant my thoughts loosened,
and took off like the owls that circled overhead,
and I knew your hands would later catch in my hair,
hoped the wedding ring on them never seemed a snare –
for if you were a traveller I would not make you settle,
but would have you follow your own weather,
and if you were a hawk I would not have you hooded,
but would watch, dry-mouthed, as you hung above the fields,
and if you were a rabbit I would not want you tame,
but would watch you gambolling through the bracken,
though there is dark meat packed around your ribs,
and the hawk hangs in the skies.

Kate Potts

A Fire Ceremony

The broadway's spun over in new lint snow –
    sugared, soundless. The light's leached of its prism tones.

The air's a first, stark, catch in the jarring pipes, the morning's *'hem.*
    Like this, a gritted sheet of city could seem
fleshed at my feet, grace-noted, just, with a magpie's slow, scolding
                                       spree.

Slipped out into it we're dwarflings, unworldly,
    cannot assume the learned drill between the alarm clock's
jittery knell and the end – the nine-to-five
    that chromes by in blinked jags.

Horizon camouflages against the clouds like a whitening, sea-to-sky
                                         melt.
    We guess at distances, observing birdflight. Only the sound
of caws carries, the scrum and dragging of stuck tyres.
    Our veins thrum to the whiteout's mesmer, the sacerdotal drone.

When quick dark underlines the snow-stacked terraces, their quartz
    of knitted ice, we trek with rucksacks to the swimming pool
to find its sauna room. We plump our arses on the sweated wood.

The coals sigh, weird us with their shocks of summer heat.
    Meteors, little suns, pulse in our platelets, and in our bones.

Craig Raine

For Pat Kavanagh

dark steps
across this pale grass
perfect with dew,

dark steps
so early, so swift,
the short length of this long lawn…

Peter Reading

EXPONENTIAL

The corn-coloured neutral combine –
   first we see is its shadow
   approaching, swathing hectares.

All things in season: steady thresh,
the dark swift coming and going,
   Dow-Jones average, fin., fin.

Ed Reiss

Ka'aba

The cuboid, swathed
in black brocade
is imageless:
an empty space

you might approach
as if it marked the spot
where Adam first gave thanks
after leaving Eden

where the merchant
cupped his palm around
the Virgin and her child
to spare them from destruction

where the moon descended
circled seven times
and passing through the Prophet split
to reappear as moon

Oliver Reynolds

HODGE

for Alan Vaughan Williams

The more I think of Hodge
the more he comes to mind:
the prompt-corner ledge
curlicued with peel and rind;

his barn-door smile; his gloom;
the walk-in cupboard in the pit
he dubbed his dressing-room;
the way he always spat

and polished the leather
between sole and heel,
'Watch and learn, Oliver –
no bull like army bull…';

the way he was there and not there,
watching in the wings for hours,
then ghosting on; his flop of hair
as he bowed and gave flowers.

Robin Robertson

STRINDBERG IN SKOVLYST

I

A manor house in ruin. It suits me
down to the ground.
A tower to write in,
three rooms for the family, with a kitchen,
and all for fifty crowns a month.
Unbelievably filthy, I have to say: everything
broken, unfinished, abandoned.
In the yard, two floors below,
a mongrel half-heartedly
mounts a greyhound; blue flies
are hatching in the dung.
It fits my mood.
Wherever you look: neglect, failure,
all the shit you could wish for.
A home away from home.

They laid on quite a show, trying
to get us to take the place:
goblets of flaming spirits, the Countess
with a hurdy-gurdy, lying on the floor;
her steward as circus-master, conjurer,
with his not-so-beautiful assistant,
the blonde fat girl in a spangled costume.
All the usual card tricks, which I knew,
but then he got her up to the ceiling on poles
then whipped them away – and she stayed there,
in the air, levitating above us. And she didn't fall.

I gave them three months' rent after that, up front.

II

The Countess is mad – today and every day –
quite mad, and this is her menagerie;
the cattle and horses stay outside, eating thatch,
but the rest are residents:
cats, poultry, eight huge dogs.
She carries a white lamb, sometimes,
but her favourite is Sky-Leaper, the blind,
ancient cockerel she dandles on her lap.
Like magic, rabbits
hop out of coal scuttles,
turkeys squabble in the bathtub, eating soap.
With a flourish, she reveals
a litter of white kittens in a drawer
then, shyly,
from the front of the sky-blue
off-the-shoulder dress she wears each day,
she pulls a duckling.
A pigeon flies through the window,
followed by the male, who ambles
after her, blowing his crop, dragging
his spread tail through the dirt.
An unearthly screech, then the stately
step of an Indian peacock,
rustling down the corridor
towards the room
where two Great Danes
are standing on the shaky bed, coupling.
Speaking of which, here's Hansen,
her steward (and more than that, I suspect):
a black-fingered trickster with his
wagging forelock and dice for eyes,
up and about, flaunting
his yellow suit, the peacock feather in his hat.
And behind him, the maid – who I take
for his sister – Martha Magdalene:
sixteen if she's a day, blonde *knullhår*,

barely decent with her predatory mouth
and her dress a size too small.

A three-hander, then, with this
shambles for a stage: this home to pestilence,
cluster flies, blowflies, men and women,
Armageddon – a crucible
for turning baseness into gold.
In my head, when the gales are riding wild,
I steer towards catastrophe
then write about it.

III

*Interior. The upper rooms. Noise of children. Dim summer
sunlight through the grimy, curtainless windows. The
playwright's wife is boiling sheets, swabbing the floor-
boards with bleach.*

*Interior. Kitchen. The walls and ceilings black with soot,
the tables piled with unwashed dishes, rotting food. A side of
mutton hangs from a hook on the wall, just high enough to
be out of reach of the dogs. The maid, Martha, is shelling
peas.*

*Exterior. The pavilion on the lake. The steward, Hansen,
and the playwright in animated conversation, drinking
schnapps.*

I confess, with a clink of glasses,
to six months' celibacy at the hand
of Artemis, my wife, cruel goddess of chastity,
but he doesn't understand.
That I hate women but desire them –
hate them *because* I desire them.
The power they have.
That fear I might go mad.

That I am, already, mad.
He sighs, and tells me his ridiculous stories,
shows me conjuring tricks,
sings the same song over and over again.
I only listen when he shares his hopes
for advancement – the dream of climbing
to the top of the high tree
to rob the nest of its golden egg –
but how the trunk is too smooth to gain purchase,
and the branches too high to catch hold.

*Exterior. Garden. The Countess and the playwright walking
between the vegetable plots, overgrown with burdock and
nettles, cobbled with turds.*

She was going on about her animals, her family,
how she loved them more than any human.
And I thought of that pack of feral dogs –
vile scavengers – and all the rest of them:
the tettered, emaciated beasts.
She said she dreamed she was on top of a high pillar
and all she wanted was to fall.

Interior. The tower room. Midnight.

The girl, at my door again. What was I to do
against those lead-grey eyes, the tousled hair,
that young, thick body? That *mouth*?
The bestial ruin stinking in my face.
The snort and rut coming closer.
I ran my thumb down the seam,
opening up the velvet,
to nudge the hard pod of the bean.
She kissed me, like a cat.
Cats kill you at the throat, so I was quickly
over her, and in. Behind the trees
a thin filament of lightning briefly glowed

and died. Manumission.
And now: the fall.

IV
The voices in my head are company at last
in these high rooms
in the glove of the night, under a fretted moon.
That gypsy Hansen's out there with a gun
shouting about 'corrupting a minor' and
'raping my sister'. Letting off shots.
I was on her *once*
and all I got was scabies, and now scandal.
I told the Countess that her lover's
just a common thief;
she said, 'My brother, you mean.'

Our bags are packed.
The carriage waits below.
I have stoked the fever enough to spark some fire.
It's dreadful, I tell myself, but there's no other way.
We are above such people.
We're devoured by our own desires, our dogs,
but we survive to make art.
I am not yet forty. And now I have my play.

Notes

In the summer of 1888, Strindberg rented rooms with his wife, Siri von Essen, and
their children in the manor house at Skovlyst, near Copenhagen. The marriage
had collapsed but the family was still travelling together around Europe. In exile,
Strindberg had recently fallen heavily under the influence of the writings of
Nietzsche. During the summer in Skovlyst, he wrote – among other things – *Miss
Julie*. The poem incorporates lines and images from the play and a sentence from a
contemporary letter to Verner von Heidenstam.

knullhår (Swedish, pronounced *knool-hoer*) a neologism, literally 'fuck-hair',
suggestive of dishevelled, post-coital tangles.

Omar Sabbagh

UNCERTAINTY

Joseph K, i.m.

A small heartless cry
that gives no sound to cherishing
that has no middle nor
melody;
        the cry
of a twig crunched in dead
yellow grass, lungless and unshriven;
the heavy mantel of widowhood
it veils, like a weak bird's lost crutch:
Sadness without the light
of morning.

Carole Satyamurti

TERROR

Now the Shabanites are living in our city
you can't be too careful.
They're everywhere.

What does a Shabanite look like?

Like anyone – friendly, shakes your hand
but you soon know you've met one.

How?

Your skin starts to burn and crack. I've heard
one man's hand shrivelled and fell off.

Have you ever seen one?

I might have – you never know
who's standing next to you.
A few months back, my cousin's sister-in-law
was queuing for fish. The man behind
smiled at her – and she realised, and ran!

*What if you never look a stranger in the eye,
what if you keep your hands in your pockets?*

I told you – they're everywhere.
Your dentist might be one,
the check-out girl, poisoning your change.

*But didn't I hear they tracked down
the last Shabanite – beat him to death?*

Well, but what about the Shakuni? I'm told
they operate in cells, have horrible cold breath.
They're everywhere.

Jean Sprackland

Shepherdess and Swain

Cremated bones go into china,
and it is too brittle you would think for these
come-hither folds of cloth with all their warm suggestions.

He has one knee on the blue-and-white ground
and the other pressed to her skirt.
He raises one badly painted eyebrow.
She urges him on from the corner of a smudged mouth.
His hand is on his racing heart.
She is reaching to touch his arm.
And the dew rises through them.

No, it is the wrong stuff: all gloss
and deadpan, suitable for vases and teapots.
There is dust in all its clefts and curlicues,
and tapped with a fingernail it makes a cold note.

This belongs on a mantelpiece in a dismal sitting room
where the chimney will not draw; where someone
bored with a lifetime of unheard melodies
would come in and pick it up

and look at the boy cross-eyed with lust
and the poor girl flushed and impatient,
the two of them trapped in this rictus of desire

and no release, no way to pitch the story on
except to knock them onto the hearth and smash them.

Matthew Sweeney

SHIPWRECKED

The Spanish soldier stood on the beach at Ballyliffin,
he had managed to swim ashore from the sinking ship –
the last windblown straggler of the failed Armada –
and he eyed, at the far end of the strand, a castle,
wondering what nobleman lorded it there, and whether
a servant was peering at him now through a telescope.
Were dogs loping their way to him across the sand?
He was renowned in Burgos for his manner with hounds,
and he had some English, but they spoke Irish here.
Had he escaped drowning to be hacked to pieces, then
devoured by a pack of Irish wolfhounds? He wished
he had a box of the gold bars that had been on the ship –
they would have bought him any amount of armour.
He looked around for rocks to hide behind and wait –
for what? There would be no rescue from Spain, nor
from any of these indigenous Irish – although he was
here to help them defeat the brutal, Protestant English,
but what help could he deliver alone? Still, hadn't those
at home welcomed the exiled Donegal prince, O'Donnell,
and named a long avenue in central Madrid after him?
And hadn't they sent a whole Armada to help the Irish?
No one could have factored in such a huge storm.
How many, like him, stood on a windy, northern beach,
wondering what could be in store for them? He wished
he'd done research and knew the word for *hungry*,
if nothing else. He wished he'd done a course in Irish.
He'd heard that Irish girls were the lookers of Europe.
Maybe he'd get lucky and a beauty would rescue him?

Brian Turner

Puget Sound

Clouds shield the stars where jellyfish
drift in the harbor, and facing the water,
in an idling Chrysler, windshield
glazed by rain, Private Reynolds,

who in six weeks will deploy to Iraq
for the first time, white-knuckles
the cord, the ends wrapped tight
around each hand. His wife stops breathing –
her larynx exhausted within a tunnel of light.

Daybreak. Workday. Night.
For four days she drifts in the Sound.
Barges ferry lumber to the pulp mill
and dockside fishermen cast lines
for rock cod and eel. Joggers,
mothers pushing strollers, teens
on rollerblades listening to music
through headphones – all pass by.
A golden retriever named Pepper
discovers her – a woman with eyes
mirroring the sea, washed and transformed,
grayed-out by what she's seen.

Eoghan Walls

Osiris and the Prague Flood

Watching the fertile but flat and watery landscape passing –
I thought of how we had laughed bewildered as teenagers
returning from a night of wine with Christians – at how
they could smile at us but know us damned forever –
in a river of fire with pagans forever mute to God –
and now that my relationship had ended – the bad sex
and the lack of sex – the meals where both of us wished
to be sat at other tables – eat from lives not yet our own –

and coming to see you had been a part of that – escape –
not seen since I'd left with two Czech girls – they camped
with me beside a river – past tragic tussles in a two man tent –
but meeting you in Pizza Ovenecka – with your young wife –
so beautiful and new and Catholic – and you with God
now finally – the wine tasted wrong or odd and we knew –
something was amiss – was it the weather of those days –
or would the blood of Christ be stale till I had left you –

and the television showed the national signs of this unrest –
the flood was moving down towards the city – small towns
allowed their banks to break to stop the flow – it did not stop –
old women lifted by helicopter from the roofs of houses –
men boating down the streets they'd always lived in –
and the bars we went to in the pauses – leaving your wife
to wrap up blankets for the council – were empty –
and my book of poems was nearly empty – and our talk –

as the city filled to the brim with water – overspill –
in the darkness on the Charles Bridge – jazz bands replaced
by rain and the flash of sirens – the stories – the elephant
shot in his cage – the overwash of buried chemicals – the priest
who stood and said his mass despite the kneehigh depth of water –
the ten-thousand-dollar chair swept from the gallery

like so much jetsam – the seal that left the zoo – escaped –
to end up poisoned when the Voltova became the Elba –

how silt would end up thick across the cobbles – the stains
on buildings – the cars now washed away – the grubby silence
that would haunt the city – and as we stood in darkness –
sharing an umbrella with your sister – I knew I could not
place my hand on hers – thinking of Osiris far from home –
watching the flooding of the Nile without his penis –
and you looking at me through the rain – as if all my teeth
had fallen out – and I was calling out for this destruction.

Heidi Williamson

SHOE, 1979

I have this image of me
that's almost the picture:
gap grin, hedge hair, stripy-tee,
with long childish bones,
on a log bench raised in a river,
West Acre, the 1970s.
My legs are dangling in the flow,
arms angled, clinging on,

I'm surrounded by relatives.
And some time before or after
the shutter snapped,
my white jelly shoe slipped
into the murk below.
I couldn't retrieve it.
Even if somehow it was there now,
it must have grown out of me.

Anna Woodford

Looking Back

If I could
I'd go back
and slide my tongue
out your mouth.
I'd pick up a tissue
and mop my damp praise
from your neck and your chest.
I'd take my pound of flesh
back. If there was a master tape
of our night
I'd get my hands on a copy
and set it to rewind,
so I could watch our bodies
unmaking love,
remaking the bed.
I'd leave nothing to chance.
I'd backtrack us all the way
out the bedroom
and into the lounge
and I wouldn't pause there
to pick up my coffee.

Adam Wyeth

PINTER'S PAUSE

(for Paula)

It was the height of summer.
We sat in the garden reading a play.
I played him and you played her.
Before long you said, 'Do you know about
Pinter's pause? – those silent moments –
pregnant with words unsaid…'

I wasn't really listening, I thought I saw
a fox in the undergrowth –
stopping by the hedge to eye up his purple gloves.
Everything was in flower.
We read the play right the way through.
I was him, she was you.

Looking up during each pause –
I imagined him creeping beyond our garden
wriggling under the gap in the fence
behind the clematis and convolvulus –
or whatever it was? The twist of hedgerow,
the turn in the lane, the height of the day.

Just then, everything stopped,
caught between the hands of a clock.
The sun was at its zenith;
I thought if I put my hand out,
I could catch it and put it in my pocket.
I didn't want to say anything, to break the spell.

Then it moved on –
like a great cog in a grandfather clock.
The season was passing,
our lives were turning before its eyes.
Those soft paws padding the undergrowth,
gingerly treading between the hedgerows –
beyond the clematis and convolvulus

Publisher acknowledgements

Fergus Allen · CLOUD · *Before Troy* · CB Editions

Rachael Boast · FIRE SHOWER · THE HUM · *Sidereal* · Picador Poetry

Eavan Boland · RE-READING OLIVER GOLDSMITH'S 'THE DESERTED
VILLAGE' IN A CHANGED IRELAND · PN Review

Judy Brown · THE SOUVENIRS · TWO VIRGINS · *Loudness* · Seren

Alan Brownjohn · HIS CLASSIC MODESTY · *Ludbrooke & Others* ·
Enitharmon

John Burnside · ON THE FAIRYTALE ENDING · NATIVITY · *Black Cat Bone* ·
Cape Poetry

Diane Cockburn · ELECTRIC MERMAID IN BELL'S FISH AND CHIP SHOP ·
Electric Mermaid · Arrowhead Press

Wendy Cope · AT STAFFORD SERVICES · *Family Values* · Faber and Faber

Ian Duhig · THE ORIGIN OF PESTILENCE · *Pandorama* · Picador Poetry

Michael Egan · THREE ITALIANS AND A SPANIARD · *Steak & Stations* ·
Penned in the Margins

Mark Ford · RAVISHED · *Six Children* · Faber and Faber

Annie Freud · LUST · *The Mirabelles* · Picador Poetry

Nancy Gaffield · 27 KAKEGAWA · 45 ISHIYAKUSHI · *Tokaido Road* ·
CB Editions

Lavinia Greenlaw · THE DRIP TORCH · *The Casual Perfect* ·
Faber and Faber

Kelly Grovier · THE GUEST · *The Sleepwalker at Sea* · Oxford Poets

David Harsent · THE LONG WALK TO THE END OF THE GARDEN ·
THE HUT IN QUESTION · *Night* · Faber and Faber

Geoffrey Hill · 13 · 32 · *Clavics* · Enitharmon

Alan Jenkins · SOUTHERN RAIL (THE FOUR STUDENTS) · Poetry Review

Fawzi Karim · AT THE GARDENIA'S ENTRANCE · *Plague Lands and other
poems* · Carcanet

August Kleinzahler · EXILES · London Review of Books

R F Langley · TO A NIGHTINGALE · London Review of Books

Gwyneth Lewis · OCEAN WAVES · *Sparrow Tree* · Bloodaxe Books

Tim Liardet · '...LAY THEE DOWN' · *The Storm House* · Carcanet

Michael Longley · THE WREN · CLOUDBERRIES · *A Hundred Doors* ·
Cape Poetry

Peter McCarey · GLYPH · *Collected Contraptions* · Carcanet

David Morley · CAMARGUES · *Enchantment* · Carcanet
Les Murray · HIGH-SPEED BIRD · *Taller When Prone* · Carcanet
Daljit Nagra · A BLACK HISTORY OF THE ENGLISH-SPEAKING PEOPLES ·
Tippoo Sultan's Incredible White-Man-Eating Tiger Toy-Machine!!! ·
Faber and Faber
D Nurkse · THE MIDDLE OF THE FOREST · INVENTING NATIONS · *Voices over Water* · CB Editions
Sean O'Brien · JOSIE · LEAVETAKING · *November* · Picador Poetry
Bernard O'Donoghue · VOCATION · *Farmers Cross* · Faber and Faber
Sharon Olds · SONG THE BREASTS SING TO THE LATE-IN-LIFE BOYFRIEND ·
Poetry London
Ian Pindar · WHAT IS THE MATTER? · *Emporium* · Carcanet
Clare Pollard · THE CARAVAN · *Changeling* · Bloodaxe Books
Kate Potts · A FIRE CEREMONY · *Pure Hustle* · Bloodaxe Books
Craig Raine · FOR PAT KAVANAGH · *How Snow Falls* · Atlantic Books
Peter Reading · EXPONENTIAL · *Vendange Tardive* · Bloodaxe Books
Ed Reiss · KA'ABA · *Your Sort* · Smith/Doorstop
Oliver Reynolds · HODGE · *Hodge* · Areté Books
Robin Robertson · STRINDBERG IN SKOVLYST · London Review of Books
Omar Sabbagh · UNCERTAINTY · *My Only Ever Oedipal Complaint* ·
Cinnamon Press
Carole Satyamurti · TERROR · *Countdown* · Bloodaxe Books
Jo Shapcott · BEES · Poetry Review
Jean Sprackland · SHEPHERDESS AND SWAIN · The North Magazine
Matthew Sweeney · SHIPWRECKED · Wasafiri
Brian Turner · PUGET SOUND · *Phantom Noise* · Bloodaxe Books
Eoghan Walls · OSIRIS AND THE PRAGUE FLOOD · *The Salt Harvest* · Seren
Ahren Warner · JARDIN DU LUXEMBOURG · ABOUT SUFFERING THEY WERE
NEVER WRONG, THE OLD MASTERS... · *Confer* · Bloodaxe Books
John Whale · WHISTLEJACKET · LINES ON THE DEATH OF MARY
WOLLSTONECRAFT · *Waterloo Teeth* · Carcanet/Northern House
Nerys Williams · THE DEAD ZOO, DUBLIN · LOIE FULLER'S DANCING SCHOOL ·
Sound Archive · Seren
Heidi Williamson · SHOE, 1979 · *Electric Shadow* · Bloodaxe Books
Anna Woodford · LOOKING BACK · *Birdhouse* · Salt Publishing
Adam Wyeth · PINTER'S PAUSE · *Silent Music* · Salmon Poetry